Dedicated to Jane Anne Wickiser

RALPH L. WICKISER

THE REFLECTED STREAM

THE ABSTRACT YEARS 1985-1998

RALPH L. WICKISER

THE REFLECTED STREAM

THE ABSTRACT YEARS 1985-1998

DAVID ADAMS CLEVELAND / WALTER WICKISER

WALTER WICKISER GALLERY, INC., PUBLISHER

Editor: Walter Wickiser

Designers: Misa Hoshino, Joowon Kim, & Alix Nicholaeff

Library of Congress Control Number: 2012932973

ISBN — 978-0-615-59743-0

WALTER WICKISER GALLERY, INC.
210 Eleventh Avenue, Suite 303
New York, NY 10001
www.walterwickisergallery.com
wwickiserg@aol.com

COVER IMAGE: SHADOW II, 1994, OIL ON LINEN. 40" X 60"

PAGE 2: BLUE STREAM, 1998, OIL ON LINEN, 16" X 20"

Contents

INTRODUCTION

What places Ralph Wickiser amongst the finest of American post-War artists was his ability to constantly re-invent himself decade after decade. A trick he managed in the last decade of his life by reverse-engineering his style yet again with a return to his vital roots in fifties abstraction. This final achievement completed a breathtaking arc of visual exploration that began in a representational mode in the 1930s, moved into Abstract Expressionism in the 1950s, segued into Abstract Representation in the 1970s, only to push new boundaries with his purified and simplified Analytical Abstractions of the late 1980s until his death in 1998.

How many aging artists in their seventies have the chutzpah much less the energy to move on from a sumptuous and dazzling signature style—the Reflected Stream paintings of 1975 to 1985—and further extend that vision into the often treacherous arena of two-dimensional flat abstraction? One is reminded of the aging Monet and his obsession with capturing the essence of light and form in the floating world of his lily pad ponds. Wickiser, a nature poet at heart, with a visual acuity only surpassed by Thoreau in his journals, managed in his last period to capture the scintillating evanescent light forms found on the surface of a tiny stream in Woodstock, and transform that experience into works at once symphonic and exquisitely intimate. These transfixing paintings depict a world both interior and exterior, a place of the spirit as much as the mind, where floating sumptuous fields of symbolic natural forms tantalize the beholder. Time is crystallized. Patterns of color beguile and challenge the viewer. Only a consummate craftsman in the handling and manipulation of paint could make such meticulous dissections of nature sing on the canvas.

In works such as *Soaring*, 1987 (p. 37), Wickiser has extended the capacity of the human eye to delve into the metamorphic quiddity of the natural world. By emphasizing the flattened two-dimensional color planes of mobile reflections and hard-edged natural objects, shapes at once familiar and not, the artist opened up fresh ways of seeing and experiencing the interaction of translucent light and the physical world that contains that light. This ephemeral aqueous realm of positive and negative images, where light and physical objects seem to interpenetrate, is Wickiser's true subject. These are things of ambiguity, of mystery and dream: the unseen world of the poet and shaman. In old age, with camera in hand, Wickiser would carefully make his way to a stream near his Woodstock home and spend hours watching and photographing and taking field notes. The artist was, in effect, bringing us news of a visionary world ever in the making, carefully mapping out a journey into time and space that physicists delving into string theory might well find bracing if not confounding. Back in the studio, Wickiser's real genius presented itself when, by giving us less visual information on canvas in terms of a third dimension—forgoing even heavy gestural pigment, he actually provided more information to the eye by impelling the viewer to decipher and make sense of the organic pattern-structures of interacting light and form. This delicate minuet of reflected-refracted light and the highlighted patterns that define objects in space invites the imagination to engage with the work, not unlike how a metaphor on the page unites disparate imagery into a hybrid sensation. Wickiser, spinning webs of chromatic filigree, is a poet in paint.

Color and tone is yet another strategy employed by the artist to elucidate these departures into the realm of aesthetic wonder. In *Clustered*, 1988 (p. 43), the dominant pink, purple, gray, and delft blue tonalities unify and further transform the scene into a spellbinding image of the familiar and strange. One detects in the flattened planes of color-forms elements of early modernists like August Vincent Tack and Milton Avery (a longtime friend of Wickiser), but here extrapolated and extended by the way in which the tones of the various shapes play off one another, seeming to move forward and back on the canvas surface, and so hint at yet undiscovered dimensions. Likewise, the formal dynamic of lighter and darker hues jitterbugging in close proximity keeps the canvas energized and alive with each repeated viewing. Nothing remains the same…all is aswirl with frozen motion. Similarly, *In Yellow*, 1987 (p. 45), the soothing dominant tonalities of yellow-green evoke a sylvan moment, but one of such kaleidoscopic complexity that the viewer is compelled to juggle feelings of dreamy rest with rapt fascination to solve a delightful mystery.

Ralph Wickiser's Abstract Stream paintings sing of the final chapter of an artist's life; they are the epiphany of a lifetime's devotion to the splendors of the natural world. Although photography provided a tool for conceptualizing these works, the deft skills of this master artist were the crucial ingredient to their successful execution. In the acuity of observation and the deep subjectivity of translating lived experience to canvas and paint, Ralph Wickiser taps into and extends the transcendentalist tradition of Emerson and Thoreau in ways that very few artists of his generation—or any generation—even dreamed possible.

—DAVID ADAMS CLEVELAND

David Adams Cleveland is an independent curator, art historian, and novelist, most recently author of *A History of American Tonalism*, 1880 - 1920, Hudson Hills Press, 2011.

Ralph Wickiser painting in plein air, ca. 1934

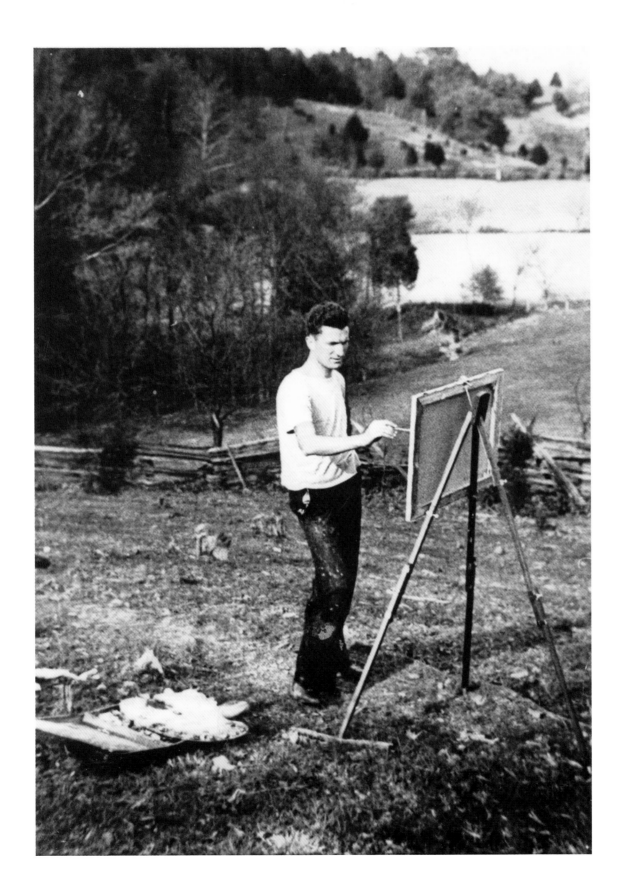

Illustrative history

BY WALTER WICKISER

Ralph Lewanda Wickiser was born in Greenup, Illinois in 1910 to Hirk and Lydia Wickiser. His family consisted of three brothers and four sisters. His middle name, Lewanda, was an Indian name. Ralph's grandparents were farmers and his father worked two jobs seven days a week. During the evening, his father worked for the Illinois Central Railroad as a telegraph operator and in the day he did painting and wallpapering. When he wasn't attending school, Ralph helped his dad and often spent his summers tending his grandfather's apple trees. In his younger years, Ralph was also a musician and sang at church-related events, such as weddings and funerals, with his friend the famous folk singer, Burl Ives. During his college years, he played guitar in a dance band. From a very early age, Ralph wanted to be an artist. The earliest known paintings are watercolors from his second grade class, which exhibited extraordinary talent at a very young age. His teachers praised and encouraged his artwork.

When Ralph was 18, he left Greenup to study at the Art Institute of Chicago, where he learned life drawing from 1928-1931. During the Depression, however, he could no longer support himself in Chicago and had to return to Greenup. At his mother's suggestion, he attended the state teachers' college at Eastern Illinois University in Charleston. There, he studied art, despite his frustration with the lack of modern art education at the time in America. During these years, a famous Brown County artist, Paul Turner Sargent (1880 - 1946) took Ralph under his wing and taught him a great deal about painting. Ralph would often accompany him to paint outdoors. He graduated with a BA in arts in 1934, and went to New York to visit Columbia University. At a friend's urging, while in New York, he went to see Hobart Nichols, director of the Tiffany Foundation which gave grants to artists to paint through their Artist-in-Residency program at its compound in Oyster Bay, Long Island, New York. The application process to the program was lengthy, and Ralph hesitated to apply.

Instead, with a couple of paintings under his arms, he went to see Mr. Nichols. Mr. Nichols was so impressed that he said, "Wickiser, I'm going to do something I've never done before and give you an immediate Artist-in-Residency with the Tiffany Foundation this summer." That summer he lived and painted in Oyster Bay. An exhibit at the well-known Grand Central Art Galleries followed in April 1934, where one of his paintings was reproduced and reviewed in *ARTnews*. This became a turning point in Ralph's life.

Earliest known work by Ralph Wickiser: watercolor from second grade, ca. 1917

Mr. Nichols wanted to send Ralph to Europe to cultivate him as a painter internationally. At the same time, the president of Eastern Illinois University contacted Ralph to inform him that he had arranged a teaching fellowship at Vanderbilt and Peabody in Nashville, Tennessee where Ralph could work on his master's degree and eventually his doctorate. Because the president had been working on obtaining the fellowship for Ralph for quite a long time, Ralph felt obligated to accept the offer.

Tiffany Artists Are Now on View At Grand Central

The Louis Comfort Tiffany Foundation presents the work of the artists who have been its guests during the past season at the Grand Central Art Galleries, 15 Vanderbilt Avenue, New York City, until November 3.

Many artists have been the guests of the Tiffany Foundation including Cathal O'Toole who was awarded the Joseph Pulitzer Traveling Scholarship of $1500, which is annually awarded to a student at the National Academy of Design, for 1934. Edmund R. Amateis, 1921 Prix de Rome winner of sculpture; Monty Lewis, awarded the Guggenheim Foundation Scholarship, Luigi J. Lucioni, Joseph Margulies, Lawrence T. Stévens, Frank Schwarz, Anna Fisher and many others.

Mr. Hobart Nichols, N. A., who is the Director of the Foundation, is very pleased with the results of this year's work and invites all those interested in the younger American artist to visit the exhibition.

Ralph Rowntree's pastels are known from being shown in his exhibition at the Macbeth Galleries a season or so ago. Among the water colors, Dean Faussett, Jared French and Lloyd Goff are represented with characteristic examples. Cathal O'Toole is here again, as are also J. B. Watrous, Theodore P. Shoudy, Prescott M. Jones, Carl Buck, Frederick Peterson, Horace Day and others, among them those who are new to gallery-goers as well as old friends.

The two paintings from this exhibition which we reproduce in this issue, are typical of the differences in temperament and technique to be found among the artist's of the Foundation. Ralph Wickiser's marine subject, illustrated above is severly restrained in upon the expert rendering of the still mood and pattern. Cathal O'Toole's life elements, carefully grouped "Conglomerate" on page 13 concentrates accentuate their values.

"STUDY NO. 1"   *By* RALPH WICKISER

This painting is included in the annual exhibition by artists of the Louis Comfort Tiffany Foundation now on view at the Grand Central Art Galleries.

Study No.1 reproduced in *ARTnews*, October 27, 1934

In 1936, Ralph married Jane Anne Bisson whom he met while attending Eastern Illinois University. Three children followed: Eric in 1942, Lydia in 1945, and Walter in 1952. He continued to exhibit his paintings and that year his work was shown at Rockefeller Center in New York. In the fall of 1936, he took a position teaching art at Louisiana State University (LSU) in Baton Rouge while simultaneously working on his PhD in philosophy at Vanderbilt and Peabody. While at Vanderbilt, he remained a very active painter and exhibitor. In 1937, he exhibited at the Studio Club in Nashville, Tennessee. From 1937-1941, his work traveled to museums throughout the country in an exhibition "A New Southern Group". The High Museum in Atlanta, Georgia, obtained one of his works for inclusion in its permanent collection. In 1938 he received his PhD in philosophy of education and aesthetics from Peabody College. The following year he had a solo show at the Grecian Gallery in New Orleans, Louisiana. Since the early 1930s, Wickiser's style of painting swayed back and forth between abstraction and representation.

Over The Hill, ca. 1934, 8" x 10", Oil on board

Wickiser made his first trip to Woodstock, New York to study color lithography with Emil Ganso in the summer of 1939. There he found a kindred spirit in the Catskill mountains, its vast spacious beauty and within the small, vibrant artists colony that was then Woodstock. It was the beginning of Ralph and Jane's summer pilgrimages to Woodstock. For the first time, the young painter was exposed to contemporary art movements and to pioneer

Abstract Expressionists including Franz Kline and Barnett Newman. An immediate camaraderie developed between Wickiser and Yasuo Kuniyoshi, who hosted a big party for the artist and Jane to introduce them to his Woodstock friends. This led to long friendships with Arnold Blanch, Paul Burlin, Rollin Crampton, Doris Lee, Eddie Millman, Milton Avery, Philip Guston, and Barnett Newman. Wickiser later invited Burlin and Kuniyoshi to LSU to lecture to the art students. Wickiser became very good friends with the painter Rollin Crampton, who was particularly close friends with Barnett Newman, and the two spent long hours together talking about art. Eddie Millman and Barnett Newman would often come over to Wickiser's Woodstock home and have discussions on painting. Wickiser warmly referred to Newman as "Barney".

Mexican Series, ca. 1940, 14" x 8", Watercolor on paper. Reflecting street life in Guadalajara and Tosco, where Ralph and Jane visited Diego Rivera

In the summer of 1940, Ralph and Jane drove from Louisiana to Guadalajara and Tosco in Mexico, where they spent time with Diego Rivera. As Jane recalls, "He was so ugly he was beautiful." The summer yielded a series of watercolors created outdoors in the marketplaces of Guadalajara and Tosco. In 1941 he was named Chairman of the Art Department at Louisiana State University in Baton Rouge.

During the war years, Wickiser enlisted as a commissioned officer in the Navy and was stationed in Washington, DC. In 1942 his work was shown at the Corcoran Gallery in Washington DC, the San Francisco Museum, and the Oakland Museum in California. The Degaldo Museum in New Orleans, presently the New Orleans Museum of Art, gave him a solo show in 1943. An exhibition of his work followed in 1944 at the Dayton Museum in Ohio, and in 1946 his work was shown at the Associated American Artist Gallery in New York. He continued to alternate between abstraction, figures, landscapes, and combinations thereof always to push the boundaries of his imagination.

Preparing for Maverick party
Wickiser painting, far left, Yasuo Kuniyoshi, middle with hat

Courtesy of the Woodstock Artists Association & MuseumArchives (above and right)

Group party at the Maverick (Wickiser, top row, third from left)
Other notables in the photo —
Philip Guston and Herman Cherry (top row second and third from right)
Yasuo Kuniyoshi (in the middle with hat), and Edward Millman (second row, third from left)

Wickiser working on lithographs

In 1946, he became a contributing editor to the *Encyclopedia of the Arts*. As a creative painter, art educator, and writer, Wickiser was keenly sensitive to the lack of good textbooks on art education. His first book, *An Introduction to Art Activities* was published by Henry Holt and Co. in 1947. The book became one of the most widely used textbooks for teachers and students of art education in colleges and universities for decades. Wickiser also coauthored *Mardi Gras Day* in 1947 with Caroline Durieux and John McCrady, two other well-known Louisiana artists. Many of his lithographs, published in the book, were inspired by photographs he had taken of Mardi Gras. It was at this point that he developed a serious interest in photography to enhance his range as an artist. That year his work was shown at the Dallas Museum in Texas, and ten of his color lithographs were reproduced in an article "The American Highway" in *The Lamp,* published by Standard Oil of New Jersey. In 1948-49, he was commissioned by Ford Motor Company for a watercolor series, which were reproduced in their magazine, *The Ford Times.* In 1948 his work was exhibited at the Library of Congress at the Annual Print Exhibition.

In The Louisiana Bayous, lithograph reproduced in *The Lamp*

Mardi Gras Day Book Signing Event
Wickiser (far left), well-known Louisiana artists, Caroline Durieux, and John McCrady

Halloween, lithograph, ca. 1948

Ralph and Jane continued to summer intermittingly in Woodstock until 1949, when they bought land there and built a house and a studio. In 1950, Wickiser hosted a conference at the Woodstock Artists Association with talks by Franz Kline, Robert Motherwell, and Yasuo Kuniyoshi. In 1951, Wickiser hosted the Fourth Annual Conference on Art at the Woodstock Artists Association with Herman Cherry, Franz Klein, Yasuo Kuniyoshi, Robert Motherwell, Barnett Newman and Ben Shawn.

Kuniyoshi worked with Wickiser on the conferences and helped organize them. In 1950, his work was shown at the Metropolitan Museum of Art in New York, and at the Pennsylvania Academy in 1951. In 1952, he had a solo show at the University of Louisville in Kentucky.

Third Woodstock Art Conference, "The Artist and the Museum", September 1st and 2nd, 1950 (Wickiser, far right) The speakers were: Philip Evergood, Lloyd Goodrich, Edith Halpert, Rene d'Harnoncourt, Hartlett H. Hayes, Jr., Yasuo Kuniyoshi, Andrew Ritchie, Francis Henry Taylor, and Hudson D. Walker.

Courtesy of the Woodstock Artists Association & MuseumArchives

From 1950 through 1968, the focus of Wickiser's paintings was non-objective. The series of paintings created were *Compassion I* (1950-1958), and *Compassion II* (1959-1968). Some of the work was inspired by Matthais Grunewald's *Isenheim Altarpiece,* which he viewed as one of the greatest artworks ever made. In the *Compassion I* paintings, he wanted to create a visual feeling of uplifting or resurrection through the use of square-shaped panels throughout the paintings and glazes.

Wickiser's work was included in the 1953 Annual Exhibition of Contemporary American Painting at the Whitney Museum with such artists as Milton Avery, Ralston Crawford, William de Kooning, Adolph Gottlieb, Philip Guston, Georgia O'Keeffe, and Jackson Pollock. In 1954, his work was exhibited at the Cincinnati Museum. He continued to exhibit at the Woodstock Artists Association and his lithographs were in a State Department traveling exhibition in Europe from 1954-1956.

Ralph Wickiser's abstract paintings from the 1950s are exemplary of that period of modernist American art; yet they also look astonishingly fresh. His great love of both materials and the act of painting is evident in the meticulously considered treatment of his surfaces, in their textures, in the balance, range and subtle modulation of colors—the elegant blues, reds shading to rose, greens, yellows, the orange burnished gold—and in many layers of glazes that give his colors their intensity and resonance, their depths. His handling of the paint alternates between thin, translucent passages which the light can penetrate and rich, heavy impasto; in some instances, the paint has been fashioned into rosette-like shapes, and abstract flowering into bas-relief. He also affixes nails, paint tubes and other painting paraphernalia to the surfaces as if to include all aspects for painting within itself. Surface, space, color, light, brushwork are all subjects, as are the grid and the band which are the dominant structuring devices though more evident in some paintings than in others. Yet despite this phenomenological approach, the surface seems to dissolve into illusion, shimmering at the edges like a mirage. Some of these canvases were inspired by Grunewald's Isenheim Altarpiece, whose mysterious, difficult colors and sharply expressive figures in the extraordinary central panel echo the sorrow and pity of the crucifixion with particular passion, particular poignancy; they then shift to more triumphant tones in other sections, juxtaposing the tragic and the joyous, the beautiful and the grotesque, the hateful and the compassionate. Ralph Wickiser's paintings would distill those emotions into color and through color, share the spirit of that profoundly human drama.

Lilly Wei

New York City, January 1996

Wickiser exhibition, LSU, ca. early 1950s

In 1956, Wickiser left LSU to direct the art education division at State University of New York (SUNY) at New Paltz. During this time, he worked on his final and most popular book *An Introduction to Art Education* published in 1957 by World Book Company. The book brought Wickiser to the forefront of American art education. While at SUNY he hired Ilya Bolotowsky to teach, and his serious interest in photography as related to painting came to full bloom. While the contractors were building his house in New Paltz, they dug up huge boulders and left them in a pile in the backyard. He photographed them meticulously taking the same frame during different times of the year. It would be more than a decade later until he returned to the photographs of the boulders and painted them in a series *The Four Seasons*. This was also the beginning of a life-long interest in rocks as being animate objects, which he continued to paint in the *Reflected Stream Series* from 1975 until the end of his life in 1998.

1953 ANNUAL EXHIBITION OF
CONTEMPORARY AMERICAN PAINTING

OCTOBER 15 — DECEMBER 6

WHITNEY MUSEUM OF AMERICAN ART
TEN WEST EIGHTH STREET • NEW YORK

Annual Exhibition of Contemporary American Painting (Oct. 15 - Dec. 6, 1953), Whitney Museum of American Art, New York, NY. Ralph L. Wickiser exhibited a painting *Number Three.*

Compassion Series - *Red and Rough I*, 1956
Oil and mixed media on canvas, 42" x 60"

17

Wickiser always wanted to live in New York City, and after a brief stint at SUNY, New Paltz, he left to Chair the Undergraduate Art Department at Pratt Institute in Brooklyn. In 1959, his works were included in exhibitions at the Brooklyn Museum, Long Island University, and the Momentum Institute of Design in Chicago. In 1962, he created the Master of Fine Arts program at Pratt Institute and subsequently became the Director of the Division of Graduate Programs in Art and Design. The new program was one of a few of its kind in the United States at that time. During that time, faculty members included Ernie Briggs, Herman Cherry, Edward Dougmore, Franz Klein, Jacob Lawrence, George McNeil, Stephen Pace, and Philip Pearlstein. Wickiser formed close personal friendships with Jacob Lawrence, George McNeil, and Stephen Pace. In a series consisting mostly of 8' by 6'

Wickiser and students at Pratt Institute (*Compassion II* paintings in the background)

paintings *Compassion II*, he continued to paint in pure abstraction; however, the work now took on more of an expressionist feeling. Exhibitions continued at the Woodstock Artists Association in 1960, 1961, 1963, and 1969, and there were exhibitions at the Main Gallery, at Pratt, in 1960, 1966, and 1968 through 1971.

In the mid 60s, Wickiser became interested in the figure again when he began regularly attending studio sessions with other faculty members. Some of the faculty members who regularly attended were George McNeil, Stephen Pace, and Philip Pearlstein. At that point, Wickiser left seventeen years of painting abstractly and went back to his semi-realistic roots from the Chicago Art Institute pre-Depression days. However, in the figurative work, there was still abstraction. This series was based on photographs of the figure that he had taken, and the main

Compassion II Series - *Eros*, 1960
Oil on linen, 84" x 72"

Wickiser in his studio Woodstock,
NY, ca. 1968

theme was vanity and the apple, probably relating to the Garden of Eden. Many of the paintings were triptychs and involved the relationship between the figure and its reflection in the mirror. This was probably the beginning of his interest in reflections, and would remain a constant theme in his paintings, using different subject matter, for the rest of his life. He continued to paint this series for approximately seven years until 1972.

In the early 1970s Wickiser turned his attention to the photographs he had taken many years before of the boulders and painted the *Four Seasons* series. The series was exhibited in 1975 at the Pacem en Terris Gallery at the United Nations in New York. In these paintings, he started to synthesize abstraction and representation using all of the elements that he had been working with since the 1930s. Wickiser's style of synthesizing representation and abstraction as well as his deep-found interest in rocks as animate objects and painting rocks would continue for the rest of his life particularly in *The Reflected Stream* series.

From a clump of boulders left by a bulldozer behind his house in New Paltz in the mid-50s, Wickiser meticulously photographed the changing light patterns of vivid textured rocks and earth, taking the identical frame at the same time each day, and transforming the images into The Four Seasons Series. Painted nearly fifteen years later, Wickiser's Four Seasons: Spring, Summer, Winter and Fall personifies the depth and breath of the philospher/painter's passion for seemingly innocuous forms of nature.

Lydia Wickiser Tortora
Long Island, NY, 1999

Four Seasons, *Spring, Summer, Fall*, and *Winter*, 1972-1976, Oil on linen, 60" x 72"

Photograph of Sawkill Stream by Ralph Wickiser ca. 1993

In 1975, Ralph and Jane retired to their house in Woodstock, NY and Wickiser was finally able to realize his lifelong dream to devote his full time to painting. It was at this point that the camera became an important tool in the discovery of his subject matter. He started photographing nature in Woodstock, especially the local streams, such as the Esophus. From this came the earliest series of his work on the stream which were primarily monochromatic. Then Wickiser discovered a little stream a couple of fields over from his studio called Vredenburg, and he began to make regular trips there to photograph. This was the beginning of his serious interest in reflections in the pools of water. There was a part of the stream with two or three pools in it and he began taking hundreds of photographs of the reflections in those pools. Because the camera could see at high-speed and freeze these moments in time, a whole new world of vision opened up to him. Photographing at the four-hundredth of a second allowed him to capture the rapid movement of the water, light, rocks, and the reflections of trees and sky.

These are images that we see as moving video, but because they are moving very fast our mind does not still-frame them. The camera allowed him to still-frame nature in all its abstraction and to paint as it actually exists. The photographs were, however, only used as reference because ultimately he would paint in colors and forms unique to his style. In his choice of subject matter in the pools of the stream, he was particularly interested in and drawn to the ugliness in nature, because as he put it, "That's where the beauty is." As time went on, his paintings of the stream became more and more a synthesis of representation and abstraction.

During the 1960s and 1970s, he was included in the *Blue Book*, *Who's Who in America*, *Who's Who in the United States*, *Who's Who in American Art*, *Who's Who in the East*, *The National Register of Prominent Americans & International Notables*, *The New York Art Year Book*, and numerous other publications. In 1974 and 1978, he had exhibitions at Harriman College in Harriman, NY. In 1976 and 1978, Wickiser exhibited at the Lotus Gallery, one of Soho's first galleries. In 1977, his works were included at Nassau County Community College in Long Island, NY. In 1978, works were included in Ulster County Community College. Throughout the 1980s his works were shown in galleries in Boston, New York, and Washington, DC.

Photograph of Vredenburg Stream by Ralph Wickiser ca. 1983

Ralph and Jane Wickiser in front of Gallery 630 B,
New Orleans, LA, 1990

George McNeil and Jane Wickiser at Z Gallery, 1991

Beginning in 1985, Wickiser's paintings of the stream begin to evolve into a purer form of abstraction. This marked a radical departure from the stream as he had painted it from 1975 to 1985. From 1985 until his death in 1998 the stream continued to be a source of inspiration and synthesis of representation and abstraction.

In 1990, Wickiser returned to New Orleans, Louisiana, to exhibit at Gallery 630 B. It was a sentimental journey for my mom, dad, and me after an absence of almost thirty-five years. Wickiser received a heart-felt welcome home as a Louisiana artist. That year, I also became a director of one of the first galleries in America from mainland China, the Z Gallery in New York City and Wickiser showed there with painters of the Star Star Group from Beijing. Eventually, I opened my own gallery in Soho, NY in 1992, and held several exhibitions where Wickiser was reunited in show with his old friends, George McNeil, and Stephen Pace. In 1993, Wickiser exhibited at the Haenah Kent Gallery in Soho, NY, and in 1994 he exhibited at the Haenah Kent Gallery in Seoul, Korea. In 1997, there was a solo exhibit of his work at The Gallery at the Roundabout Theatre in Times Square, NY. Several television programs were made by Images Art, New York, and shown on Manhattan and Paragon Cable Television Channels. During the 1990s, his exhibits were reviewed by *ARTnews*, *Art in America*, *The New York Times*, *Asahi Art Pictorial*, Tokyo, Japan, and *Art Vision*, Tokyo, Japan.

Crowd at Ralph's Opening at Z Gallery, 1991

Claude Monet tended and obsessively painted his Japanese water garden in Giverny and Frederic Edwin Church laid claim on canvas to the magnificent vistas of the Hudson River and launched an art movement in its name. These true stories, like Cézanne's penchant for ripe fruit and Degas' for bathers, have entered the pantheon of art history.

Photograph of Vredenburg Stream
by Ralph Wickiser, ca. 1978

The cumulative gaze of those legendary artists of the late 19th and early 20th centuries continues today with the abstract landscapes paintings by the octogenerian New York artist Ralph Wickiser. Since the mid-1970's Wickiser has relentlessly painted a seemingly innocuous stream (The Vredenberg Brook) behind his home and studio in the bucolic township of Woodstock.

It is challenging to imagine that such a narrow stretch of crystal clear water could occupy the brush and musing intellect of a major figure in American art education, whose roots are deeply associated with the rise of American Modernism. But over and over, like a secret mantra, Wickiser has mined images from this modest stream (photographing changing light conditions amidst the armada of color-flecked rocks and grasses) producing painting after painting.

Purple Rocks from 1996 is a haiku of painterly forms. The initial impressions from high-speed film are transformed into lyrical abstractions that can just as easily resemble the terrain as seen from weather satellite photography. Reflections of the beautifully shaped rocks skitter off the canvas, supplying the viewer with a rich cluster of grand illusions. One thinks briefly of the Surrealist-influenced Rothko as well as the alien beachscapes of Yves Tanguy. But it is pure Wickiser, contemplating and constructing another jewel-like facet of his beloved (albeit, excessively examined) stream.

Judd Tully
New York City, March 1997

Stephen and Pam Pace with Ralph Wickiser at Walter Wickiser Gallery,
Soho, NY, April, 1997
Purple Rock, 1996, Oil on linen, 40" x 60"

(Left to Right) Ralph, Stephen Pace, Walter Wickiser,
and Judd Tully at Ralph's Opening in 1997, Soho, NY

Around 1987, looking for new ideas Wickiser began photographing his apple trees which he covered with cheese cloth to keep the birds from eating the apples. Like a beautifully draped human, the light patterns and reflections of the limbs and leaves created a whole new world which Wickiser continued to paint for the ensuing years.

Photograph of Covered Apple Tree taken by Ralph, Woodstock New York, 1988

Ralph loved the apple tree he planted on the hill in 1950. For forty-eight years, he watched it grow from a spindly little seedling into a large beautiful tree. Every color of earth and sky glowed at sometime, somewhere in the apple tree. He was fascinated by the tree's infinite variety of patterns: the sunlight, the shadows, the leaves, the blossoms, the fruit, the branches, the colors, its movement when he covered the tree with cheesecloth to protect the fruit from the birds. Then, the branches really danced in the wind, and there was music.

Jane Wickiser
Bearsville, New York, February 2000

Covered Apple Tree, 1994, Oil on linen, 40" x 50"

In 1996, Wickiser became interested in the varied shapes and patterns on the grass created by the reflected shadows of our backyard trees in Woodstock. This was the last series that he would work on but he continued to work on all three series, *The Reflected Stream*, *The Covered Apple Tree* and *Shadows on the Grass* simultaneously during the last years.

He continued to walk the 200-foot, grass-worn path to his studio to paint as he had done for the past thirty-nine years up until three months before he passed away in October, 1998.

—WALTER WICKISER, 2009

Photograph of shadows on the grass taken by Ralph, Woodstock, NY, 1997

Front Lawn, 1997, Oil on linen, 26 x 34

Ralph at Vredenburg stream in Woodstock with his camera, ca. 1978

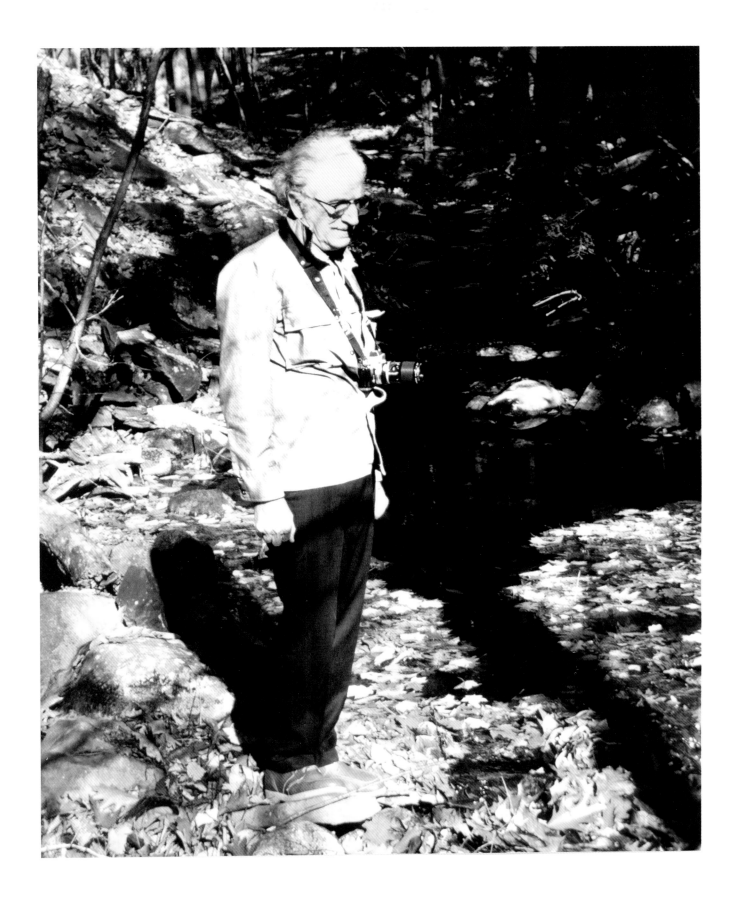

THE VRENDENBURG STREAM 1985-1990

As an abstract painter, the beauty of Nature became an irresistible lure when I moved to Bearsville, NY. After discovering the Vredenburg Stream, I was drawn in particular to a part of the stream about a city block long. Constantly changing shapes and colors found in the reflections of the stream intrigued me and in attempts to capture fleeting and momentary qualities, I focus on different depths in the stream and there I discovered a whole new world of shapes, forms, textures and colors.

Reflections are the continuous theme in all these works and the study of reflections in the stream has led to a discovery of a whole new class of art qualities in form and substance, which has allowed me to express more succinctly my appreciation of the grandeur in nature.

Ralph L. Wickiser
Woodstock, New York, 1985

Photograph of the Vredenburg stream in Woodstock, NY by Ralph Wickiser, ca. 1978

WANDERING WAVES, 1987, OIL ON LINEN, 40" X 60"

Fluttering, 1987, Oil on Linen, 30" x 50"

GREEN AND RED, 1986, OIL ON LINEN, 36" X 50"

Soaring, 1987, Oil on Linen, 36" x 50"

Intersession, 1987, Oil on Linen, 40" x 50"

Hanging, 1987, Oil on Linen, 40" x 60"

UNBALANCED, 1988, OIL ON LINEN, 40" X 60"

41

CLUSTERED, 1988, OIL ON LINEN, 36" X 60"

In Yellow, 1987, Oil on Linen, 47" x 70"

Speckled, 1987, Oil on Linen, 48" x 72"

REFLECTION #1, 1987, OIL ON LINEN, 8" X 10"

FALL LANDSCAPE, 1994 OIL ON LINEN, 8" X 10"
COLLECTION OF HIRO NOZUKA, NY

REFLECTION #2, 1987, OIL ON LINEN, 8" X 10"

STREAM IN FALL, 1988, OIL ON LINEN, 18" X 18"
COLLECTION OF DR. LLOYD HARRIS, NY

EARLY MORN, 1994, OIL ON LINEN, 10" X 8"

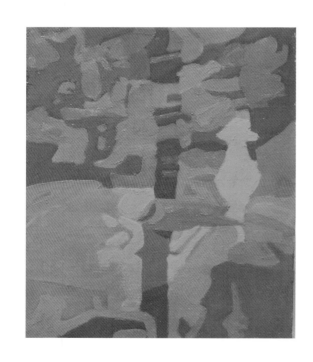

RED STREAM, 1997, OIL ON LINEN, 8" X 10"

ROSE REFLECTIONS, 1988, OIL ON LINEN, 10" X 16"

YELLOW REFLECTION II, 1987, OIL ON LINEN, 36" X 26"

THE SAWKILL STREAM 1990-1998

FALL REFLECTIONS, 1993-4, OIL ON LINEN, 10" X 14"

When Ralph turned 80 in 1990, it became difficult for him to go over and photograph the Vrendenburg stream near the house in Woodstock because the banks of the stream were very steep and dangerous. So when I would visit my parents on the weekend, we would go to photograph the stream outside Woodstock and Zena, New York. Unlike the Vrendenburg stream, which was very small with little pools of water the new stream was big and wide and this led to an evolution from the early abstract stream paintings of 1985-1990.

Walter Wickiser
New York, 2012

Photograph of Sawkill stream in Woodstock, NY by Ralph Wickiser. ca. 1993

RED REFLECTIONS, 1992, OIL ON LINEN, 34" X 45"

Interrupted, 1991-92, Oil on Linen, 30" x 50"

THE EPHEMERAL STREAM, 1992, OIL ON LINEN, 18" X 24"

Floating Rock, 1993, Oil on Linen, 16" x 20"

In Reds, 1993, Oil on Linen, 36" x 50"

GREEN STREAM, 1992, OIL ON LINEN, 30" X 50"

BLUE STREAM, 1994, OIL ON LINEN, 26" X 40"
COLLECTION OF LUCY YU FEI CHEN

REVERSE TRACING, 1995, OIL ON LINEN, 26" X 36"

THE CLUTTERED STREAM, 1992, OIL ON LINEN, 12" X 18"

SUNLIGHT SPOTS, 1992, OIL ON LINEN, 12" X 18"
COLLECTION OF DANIEL E. MUALLEM, CA

GREEN REFLECTIONS, 1995, OIL ON LINEN, 26" X 34"

THROUGH THE TREES, 1994, OIL ON LINEN, 26" X 40"
COLLECTION OF SONG JUN CHON

SUNLIGHT, 1994, OIL ON LINEN, 26" X 40"

Sunset on the Stream, 1994, Oil on Linen, 26" x 40"
Collection of George Xiong and Duoling Huang

UNTITLED STREAM, 1998, OIL ON LINEN, 26" X 36"

PURPLE STREAM, 1997, OIL ON LINEN, 26" X 34"

FANTASIA, 1997, OIL ON LINEN, 26" X 40"

UP AND DOWN, 1999, OIL ON LINEN, 8" X 10"

ROCKY LEDGE, 1998, OIL ON LINEN, 8" X 10"

WINTER REFLECTION, 1997, OIL ON LINEN, 12" X 16"

UNTITLED, 1998, OIL ON LINEN, 30" X 45"

BLACK REFLECTION, 1997, OIL ON LINEN, 24" X 40"

THE YELLOW RIVER, 1996, OIL ON LINEN, 40" x 60"

PURPLE ROCKS (FLOATING ROCKS), 1994-96, OIL ON LINEN, 40" X 60"

WHITE ROCK, 1996, OIL ON LINEN, 30" X 50"

WIND SONG, 1996, OIL ON LINEN, 26" x 40"

93

Rock Midstream, 1995, Oil on Linen, 40" x 60"
Collection of Kathy Surace-Smith, WA

DARK RIVER BOTTOM, 1997, OIL ON LINEN, 40" X 60"

Red Stream II, 1997, Oil on Linen, 40" x 60"

BROWN AND PINK, 1997, OIL ON LINEN, 40" X 60"

101

PINK REFLECTIONS, 1997, OIL ON LINEN, 40" X 60"

103

EVENING, 1997, OIL ON LINEN, 40" X 60"

RED STREAM, 1997, OIL ON LINEN, 40" X 60"

FLOATING IN THE STREAM, 1997, OIL ON LINEN, 40" X 60"

LIGHT AND DARK, 1997, OIL ON LINEN, 24" X 40"

TREES REFLECTED, 1997, OIL ON LINEN, 18" X 22"

DARK STREAM, 1997, OIL ON LINEN, 40" X 60"

SHADOWS ON THE STREAM, 1997, OIL ON LINEN, 36" X 50"

SHADOW OF A TREE, 1994, OIL ON LINEN, 14" X 18"

FADING LIGHT, 1998, OIL ON LINEN, 36" X 50"

SHADOW I, 1994, OIL ON LINEN, 40" X 60"

SHADOW II, 1994, OIL ON LINEN, 40" X 60"

SELECTED BIBLIOGRAPHY

PERIODICALS

1934   "Tiffany Artists Are Now on View at Grand Central". *ARTnews,* October 27, 1934.

Devree, Howard. "In the Galleries: Rowlandson to Fledglings". *The New York Times.*

1936   "In One-Man Exhibit Here". *The Nashville Tennessean,* May 16, 1936.

Cole, Frances. "Wickiser Exhibit at Studio Club Show Wide Variety". Nashville, TN.

"Symposium in Fine Arts to Be Held". Baton Rouge, LA: *The Reveille,* July 24, 1936.

"Tennessee Paintings, Ten by Nashvillians, on Way to N.Y. Show". Nashville, TN.

1937   "Club Speaker Says America Must Have Own Expressive Art". Marfeesboro, TN: *Women's Features-Society,* January 2, 1937.

1939   "Girl in A Doorway by Ralph Wickiser". *The Times-Picayune New Orleans States,* November 12, 1939.

Amrine, Mike. "N.O. Is Reaching Maturity In Art As 8 Shows Open in 3 Galleries". December 3, 1939.

1940   Jenkins, Jerry. "Works of Wickiser Shown in Exhibition". May 15, 1940.

"Wickiser's Etching to be Shown Sunday". Canton, NY, May 22, 1940.

1941   "'Girl at Mirror' in the Making". February 22, 1941.

"Wickiser Show". Baton Rouge, LA: *Morning Advocat*e, March 30, 1941.

"L.S.U. Artists to Exhibit Work at Three Shows". Baton Rouge, LA, April 13, 1941.

"Two Little Theaters Plan 1941 Season - L.S.U Shows Have Variety". Baton Rouge, LA, September 14,1941.

"Wickiser Named New Art Head at University". Baton Rouge, LA: *Morning Advocate,* September 14, 1941.

"Two Positions Filled on L.S.U Faculty". New Orleans, LA: *Times-Picayune,* September 15, 1941.

"Dr. R. Wickiser Heads University Art Department". Baton Rouge, LA: *State Times,* September 15, 1941.

"Chairman". New Orleans, LA: *Times Picayune,* September 15, 1941.

"Southern Group Members to Be on Hand for Opening of Art Exhibit at L.S.U. Today". Baton Rouge, LA, October 12, 1941.

"Southern Group Opens Exhibit", October 14, 1941.

"Dr. Wickiser, Lecturer Art League Exhibition". New Orleans, LA: *The Times-Picayune,* October 16, 1941.

"Southern Group Will Meet As New Art Exhibit Opens". New Orleans, LA: *The Times-Picayune,* October 19, 1941.

"L.S.U. Art Classes to Be Open for Visitors; Southern Exhibit Up". Baton Rouge, LA: *Morning Advocate.*

"40 Local Artists Are Included in Show of Art Commission". Baton Rouge, LA: *Morning Advocate.*

"Wickiser Exhibit at Southwestern". Baton Rouge, LA: *Morning Advocate.*

1942   "Wickiser Painting to Continue Tour". New Orleans, LA: *The Times-Picayune,* February 22, 1942.

"Wickiser Paints with Prolific Brush". Baton Rouge, LA: *The Summer Reveille,* August 18,1942.

1943   Darling, W. M. "Pen, Chisel and Brush". New Orleans, LA: *The Times-Picayune,* March 14, 1943.

1946   "Wickiser's Lithograph Takes High Award in the Fifth Annual Louisiana Artists Show Here". Baton Rouge, LA: *State-Times,* May 14, 1946.

"Orleans Artists Show Best Work". New Orleans, LA: *The Times-Picayune,* May 15, 1946.

"Halloween Fun". Baton Rouge, LA: *State Times,* October 30, 1946.

Browne, Vivian. "Six Southern Artists to Exhibit at UC's Annual Show on Nov. 17". *The Chattanooga Times,* November 10, 1946.

1947   Harrell. "Mardi Gras Day Illustrated by Durieux, Wickiser, and McCrady". Baton Rouge, LA: *Morning Advocate.*

"The American Highway- Lithography by Ralph L. Wickiser". New York, NY: Standard Oil Company (New Jersey), 14-18, June, 1947.

1948   "Mardi Gras Gayety Fills Joyous Book". *Chicago Sunday Tribune.*

Tallant. "Mardi Gras in Pen, Brush". New Orleans, LA: *The Times-Picayune,* January, 1948.

"Jokes on the Joker". *Times-Picayune New Orleans State Magazine,* 20-21, February 8, 1948.

Wedeck, Harry E. "New Orleans Carnival". *The New York Times,* February 8, 1948.

Giloin, Aida Mumford. "Louisiana Trapper Paintings by Ralph Wickiser". Dearborn, MI: *Ford Times,* 42, February 1948.

1950   Shane, George. "Delta Artists Draw From Local Scenes". *Des Moines Sunday Register,* 1, 12, July 9, 1950.

1951   "Wickiser, W.A.A. Chairman Praises Artists' Activities". Kingston, NY: *News Leader,* September 7, 1951.

"Gift to Art Commission". Baton Rouge, LA: *Morning Advocate,*

November 19, 1951.

"Presented to Art Commission". Baton Rouge, LA: *State Times,* November, 1951.

1952   Frankfurter, Alfred. "In the Painters' Own Words". A Book Review of The Art of the Artist, *The New York Times,* January 27, 1952.

Bier, Justin. "Wickiser Work". Louisville, KY: *The Courier-Journal,* 5, 4, March 23, 1952.

1953   Rivers, Bill. "Ph.D. With a Palette". Baton Rouge, LA: *Morning Advocate Magazine,* November 29, 1953.

1954   "Art Association Opens Annual Jury Show". *Riders' Digest,* 7, March 22, 1954.

Wickiser, Ralph. "Tradition Is Guide Post to Past; Problem Is to Get Closer to Life". Woodstock, NY: *Woodstock Press,* 5, September 9, 1954.

1955   Wickiser, Ralph. "A Contemporary Painters Attitude Toward Tradition". *College Art Journal XIV,* Spring 1955.

1958   "An Introduction to Art Education". *School Arts: The Art Education Magazine,* February, 1958.

1959   "Chairman of Art Education At Pratt Institute". Greenup, IL: *Greenup Press,* August 20, 1959.

1965   "Wickiser Named as Chairman of Graduate Programs". Pratt Institute, Brooklyn, NY: *Prattler ,* May 14, 1965.

1966   Bartczak, Peter. "Wickiser: The Work and the Man". Brooklyn, NY: *Prattler.*

1968   "Pratt Director Has Exhibit At Eastern Illinois University". *New York and Brooklyn Daily,* January 24, 1968.

"Wickiser Exhibition at Eastern Illinois University"

1976   "Ralph Wickiser - Lotus". *The Village Voice,* April 19, 1976.

"ART: Wickiser - Lotus Gallery". *The New York Times,* April 24, 1976.

1977   "The Woodstock Landscape". *Woodstock Times,* December 8,1977.

1982   Combs, Tram. "Wickiser's Common Glories". *Woodstock Times,* 12. November 18, 1982.

"Ralph Wickiser: New Look in Landscape Painting". *Woodstock Times,* November 18, 1982.

1983   "Art Notes: WAA Membership Meeting". May 26, 1983.

Isaacs, Lei. "Wickiser Art UCCA Gallery". *Woodstock Times,* October 13, 1983.

"UCCA Juried Exhibition Opens New Gallery". *Woodstock Times,* December 15, 1983.

1984   "Alice Baber Estate Gives Paintings to Tarble Center". Charleston, IL: *Mid-Illinois Newspapers,* February 1, 1984.

1987   "Dialogues at WAA". *Woodstock Times,* June 18, 1987.

1990   George, Jean Craighead. "Woodstock's Wickiser Featured in Two Shows". Kingston, NY: *Sunday Freeman,* 7, December 23, 1990.

"Wickiser In the City". *Woodstock Times,* 20, December 20, 1990.

1991   Wise, Tad. "Pieces of Eight". *Woodstock Times,* August, 1991.

1992   Twine, Tinker. "Natural Man: Artist Limns Rock and Stream with Easy Grace". *Woodstock Times,* September 17, 1992.

Shine, James G. "Park West Exhibit Shows First-Class Collection". Kingston , NY: *Daily Freeman,* October 30, 1992.

1993   Shine, James G. "The Artists' Lovely World of Landscapes". Kingston, NY: *Daily Freeman,* May 28, 1993.

Shine, James G. "Gallery at Park West - The First Two Years". Kingston, NY: *The Kingston Freeman,* February 26, 1993.

"Meditations". New York, NY: *The Villager,* April 21, 1993.

1994   Raynor, Vivien. "Contemporary Variations on a Timeless Hudson Valley Theme". *The New York Times,* July 24, 1994.

1995   Nakayama, Mikiko. "Ralph Wickiser: Nature is the Most Beautiful". *New York Magazine,* 26, August, 1995.

1996   "New York Art Scene: Ralph Wickiser". Tokyo, Japan: *Asahi Art Pictoria*l, 7, February, 1996.

1996-97   Sumiko, Kaneko. Tokyo, Japan: *Art Vision,* Winter, 24-2, 76, 1996-1997.

1997   Gladstone, Valerie. "Ralph Wickiser". *ARTnews,* 166, October, 1997.

"Art Center Features Landscape Works, McEwan and Wickiser Paintings 'Massive'". Parkersburg, WV: T*he Parkersburg Sentinel*, 9, July 21, 1997.

Muller, Seth. "Study in Contrasts, Summer Exhibit Merges Realism, Abstract Art".

Bace, Bill. "Visual Culture's Living Treasures". New York, NY: *Review,* 3, May 1, 1997.

1999   Henry, Gerrit. "The Four Seasons". *Art in America,* December, 1999.

2003   Cleveland, David. "Reviews: The Reflected Stream, The Early Years 1975-1985 ". *ARTnews,* October, 2003.

2006   "Lani Tupu." Farscape.com, June 2006. Accessed January 2012: http://www.watchfarscape.com/index.php?option=com_content&task=view&id=194&Itemid=2.

2007   Arbogast, Joanne. "Lore Degenstein Gallery Presents Ralph Wickiser Exhibition". Selinsgrove, PA: *The Daily Item,* 4, November 8, 2007.

Kidd, Victoria. "Lore Degenstein Gallery Presents Ralph Wickiser Exhibition." susqu.edu, Susquehanna University, November, 2007. Accessed January 2012: http://www.susqu.edu/news/16657.asp.

2009   Greben, Deidre S., "Ralph L. Wickiser." New York, NY: *ARTnews*, June, 2009, p. 107.

2012   "Ralph L. Wickiser, One Of The Artists Presented By Walter Wickiser Gallery At Art Chicago, 2011." mapanare.com, May, 2011. Accessed January 2012: http://www.mapanare.us/10/post/2011/5/ralph-l-wickiser-presented-by-walter-wickiser-gallery.html.

"Ralph L Wickiser." The Arteur: thestarryeye network. Accessed January 2012: http://thestarryeye.typepad.com/art/2011/07/ralph-l-wickiser.html.

"Ralph Wickiser." Art in Embassies; US Department of State. Accessed January 2012: http://art.state.gov/ArtistDetail.aspx?id=164064.

Rodeiro, Jose. "Bio." Jose Rodeiro Art; rodeiro-art.com. Accessed January 2012: http://rodeiro-art.com/index.php?option=com_content&view=article&id=2&Itemid=2.

BOOKS AND CATALOGS

1952   Hunter, E. R. *Seventh Southeastern Annual Exhibition*. Exhibition Catalog. September 28- October 12, 1952, Atlanta, GA: High Museum of Art, Atlanta Art Associations.

1953   *Annual Exhibitions of Contemporary American Painting* October 15 -December 6, 1953, New York, NY: Whitney Museum of American Art.

1961   *The Author and Writers Who's Who*. London, England.

1962-63   *Dictionary of International Biography*. London, England.

1968   Watkins, Benjamin. *A Retrospective Exhibition of Paintings* Exhibition Catalog. January 7 - February 8, 1968, Charleston, IL: Paul T. Sargent Gallery, Eastern Illinois University,

1970   *The Dictionary of British and American Writers*. London, England.

1970-71   *Who's Who in America*. Chicago, IL: Marquis.

1971   *Directory of Education Specialist. Baltimore,* MD, Spring 1971.

The Author and Writers Who's Who. London, England.

The Blue Book: Leaders of the English Speaking World. London, England: *St. James Press.*

1972   *Who's Who in the United States.*

The Blue Book: Leaders of the English Speaking World. London, England: *St. James Press.*

1972-73   *The National Register of Prominent Americans & International, Notables*. Venice, FL: *Research Center.*

1973   *Dictionary of International Biography New York Art Year Book.*

Who's Who in American Art. New York, NY: *Bowker.*

The Blue Book: Leaders of the English Speaking World. London, England: *St. James Press.*

1973-75   *Who's Who*. New York, NY: *USPRS.*

Who's Who in the East. Boston, MA: *Roosevelt & Larkin.*

Who's Who in Art. *Trade Press.*

The Writer's Directory. New York, NY: *St. Martin's Press.*

1974   *Dictionary of International Biography*. London, England.

1975   *Who's Who in the United States.*

1975-76   *New York Art Year Book.*

1978   *The Blue Book: Leaders of the English Speaking World*. London, England: *St. James Press.*

1979   *The Blue Book: Leaders of the English Speaking World*. London, England: *St. James Press.*

1981   *Who's Who in American Art. Jaques Cattell Press.*

1983   *Who's Who in America*. Chicago, IL: *Marquis.*

1988   Krantz, Les. *The New York Art Review*. Chicago, IL: *American References Publishing*, 1272, 1274, 1288.

1991   Combs, Tram. *Ralph Wickiser*. Exhibition Catalog, November 16 - December 6, 1991, New York, NY: Z Gallery.

1993   *Five Artists Haenah-Kent Group Exhibition Catalog*. Exhibition Catalog. September 18 - October 13, 1993, New York, NY: Haenah-Kent Gallery.

1994   Combs, Tram. *Ralph Wickiser, The Reflected Stream and the Covered Apple Tree, Paintings 1978 - 1993*. Exhibition Catalog, New York, NY: Walter Wickiser Gallery, Inc., April, 1994.

1996   Wei, Lilly. *Ralph Wickiser, The Compassion Series, Paintings 1950 - 1956*. Exhibition Catalog. New York, NY: Walter Wickiser Gallery, Inc., January, 1996.

1997   Tully, Judd. *Purple Rocks & Then Some: Recent Abstract Landscape Paintings of Ralph Wickiser. Ralph Wickiser, The Reflected Stream 1996 - 1997*. Exhibition Catalog. New York, NY: Walter Wickiser Gallery, Inc., April, 1997.

Zevitas, Steven. *New American Paintings, NYC Artists*. Wellesley, MA: Open Studio Press, 108-109, 127, June, 1997.

2000   Tortora, Lydia. *Ralph Wickiser, The Four Seasons, Works From the 1970's*. Exhibition Catalog. New York, NY: Walter Wickiser Gallery, Inc., April, 2000.

Wickiser, Jane. *Ralph Wickiser, The Covered Apple Tree 1987 - 1998*. Exhibition Catalog, New York, NY: Walter Wickiser Gallery, Inc., April, 2000.

2003   Henry, Gerrit. *The Reflected Stream, The Early Years 1975-1985*. New York, NY: Walter Wickiser Gallery, Inc. October, 2003.

2009   Cleveland, David. *The Reflected Stream, The Early Years 1975-1985*. New York, NY: Walter Wickiser Gallery, Inc., February, 2009.

2010   Cleveland, David A., *A History of American Tonalism: 1880-1920*. New York, NY: Hudson Hills Press: 2010.

Dean, Kevin. *REAL(ists)*. Sarasota, FL: Selby Gallery, Ringling College of Art and Design, 2010.

2012   Cleveland, David. *The Reflected Stream, The Abstract Years 1985-1998*. New York, NY: Walter Wickiser Gallery, Inc., April, 2012.

AUTHOR OF THE FOLLOWING BOOKS

1946   *Encyclopedia of the Arts*. (Contributing Editor)

1947   *An Introduction To Art Activities*. New York, NY: Henry Holt and Company, Inc.

1948   *Mardi Gras Day*. with Caroline Durieux; John McCrady, New York, NY: Henry Holt and Company, Inc.

1957   *An Introduction to Art Education*. Yonkers-on-Hudson, NY: World Book Company.

VIDEO DOCUMENTARIES & TELEVISION APPEARENCES

1991   *"Five Artists Show"* at Pratt Manhattan Center, Puck Building, Soho, NY, Produced by Bill Page, Images Art, New York, Manhattan and Paragon Television

1992   *"Ralph Wickiser"*, Produced by Bill Page, Images Art, New York, Manhattan and Paragon Television

LECTURES

1946   Chattanooga Art Association

1949   Vassar College, Woodstock Art Conference - Moderator

1950   University of Florida

1951   Bard College, Conference on Art in the Liberal Arts College
New York Public Library, "In Search of the Muse"
College Art Association, "The Artist as Teacher"

1952   Michigan State University, Graduate Seminar on Art Education
Michigan Art Education Association "Art and Value"
Fourth Annual Woodstock Art Conference, "Aesthetics and the Artist"

1953   American Council of Learned Societies Conference on Art and Art Education, Washington, DC

1954   Dallas Art Education Association

1955   Stephen Austin College

1957   SUNY Potsdam, Spring Festival of the Arts

1961,63   Patterson State College

1962   New Jersey Art Education Association, Atlantic City

1963   University of Minnesota
St. Joseph's Women's College, Brooklyn, New York

1977   University of Florida at Tampa

SELECTED SOLO EXHIBITIONS

1935   Centennial Club, Nashville, TN

1936   Louisiana State University, LA
        Studio Club, Nashville, TN

1939   Gresham Gallery, New Orleans, LA

1940   Drury College, MI

1941   Southwestern University, Lafayette, LA

1943   Delgado Museum of Art, New Orleans, LA

1952   University of Louisville, NY

1954   Louisiana State University, LA

1968   *"Retrospective"*, Eastern Illinois University, Charleston, IL

1974   Harriman College, Harriman, NY

1975   Pacem en Terris Gallery, United Nations, NY

1976   Lotus Gallery, NY

1978   Harriman College, Harriman, NY

        Lotus Gallery, NY

1982   Esta Robinson Gallery, NY

1990   Gallery 630 B, New Orleans, LA

1991   Z Gallery, Soho, NY

1992   Park West Gallery, Kingston, NY

1993   Walter Wickiser Gallery, Inc., Soho, NY

1994   *"The Reflected Stream and the Covered Apple Tree"* Walter Wickiser Gallery, Inc., Soho, NY

1995   Walter Wickiser Gallery, Inc., Soho, NY

1996   *"The Compassion Series, 1950-1956"*, Walter Wickiser Gallery, Inc., Soho, NY

1997   *"Purple Rocks & Then Some, The Reflected Stream 1996-1997"* Walter Wickiser Gallery, Inc., Soho, NY

        Parkersburg Art Center, Parkersburg, WV
        The Gallery at the Roundabout Theatre, New York, NY

1998   Walter Wickiser Gallery, Inc., Soho, NY

1999   *"The Four Seasons"* Walter Wickiser Gallery, Inc., Soho, NY
        Saginaw Art Museum, Saginaw, MI

2000   *"The Covered Apple Tree Series"*, Walter Wickiser Gallery, Inc., Soho, NY

2002   *"The Reflected Stream"*, Walter Wickiser Gallery, Inc., Soho, NY

2003   Thomas Cole House, Hudson, NY
        "The Reflected Stream, The Early Years 1975 - 1985",
        Walter Wickiser Gallery, Inc., Soho, NY

2004   *"The Compassion Series, Abstract Paintings of the 1950s and the 1960s"*,
        Walter Wickiser Gallery, Inc., Soho, NY

2005   *"The Reflected Stream, The Abstract Years, 1985-1998"*
        Walter Wickiser Gallery, Inc., Soho, NY

2006   *"The Reflected Stream, The Early Years, 1975-1978"*,
        Walter Wickiser Gallery, Inc., Chelsea, NY

2007   *"Ralph Wickiser a Retrospective 1934-1998"* Susquehanna University, Selinsgrove, PA
        "Ralph L. Wickiser Paintings, 1957-1975, The Compassion Series - The Late Abstractions, 1957-1965, Vanity, Irene and the Apple, The Nude Series 1969-1975", Walter Wickiser Gallery, Inc., Chelsea, NY

2008   *"Shadows On The Grass 1996-1998"* & *"The Covered Apple Tree 1987-1998"*,
        Walter Wickiser Gallery, Inc., Chelsea, NY

2009   *"Ralph Wickiser: A Retrospective 1934-1998"* Adelphi University, Long Island, NY
        "Ralph Wickiser: A Retrospective 1934-1998", Walter Wickiser Gallery, Inc., Chelsea, NY

2010   *"Ralph Wickiser: The Four Seasons"*, Walter Wickiser Gallery, Inc., Chelsea, NY

2011   *"Ralph Wickiser: A Retrospective of the Reflected Stream: 1975-1998"*, Walter Wickiser Gallery, Inc., Chelsea, NY

2012   *"Ralph Wickiser: The Lydia Tortora Collection"*, Walter Wickiser Gallery, Inc., Chelsea, NY

SELECTED GROUP EXHIBITIONS

1934	Grand Central Galleries, New York, NY Studio Club, Nashville, TN
1936	Rockefeller Center, New York, NY
1937	Studio Club, Nashville, TN
1937-41	*"A New Southern Group"*, Traveling Exhibition, USA
1938	Friends of Art, Baltimore, MD Third National Exhibition of American Art and Fine Arts Society, NY Harrisburg Art Association, PA
1939	Detroit Institute of Fine Arts, MI
1941	Northeast Junior College, Louisiana, LA University of Minnesota, MN
1942	Corcoran Gallery, Washington DC The Print Club, Philadelphia, PA San Francisco Museum, CA Oakland Museum, CA University of Mississippi at Oxford, MS
1943	Delgado Museum, New Orleans, LA
1944	Dayton Museum of Art, OH
1946	Associated American Artists Gallery, NY University of Chattanooga, TN
1947	Dallas Museum, TX
1948	The Washington County Museum of Fine Arts, Hangerstown, ML Library of Congress Annual Print Exhibition, Washington, DC
1950	Metropolitan Museum of Art, NY
1950	Des Moines Art Center, IA
1951	Pennsylvania Academy of Art, Philadelphia, PA
1952-58	George Binet Traveling Exhibition of Religious Prints, USA
1953	Whitney Museum of American Art Annual, New York, NY
1954	Cincinnati Museum, Cincinnati, OH The Contemporaries Gallery, NY
1954-56	State Department. European Traveling Exhibition of Color Lithographs
1956	State University of New York, New Paltz, NY
1957	Woodstock Artists Association, NY
1959	Brooklyn Museum, Brooklyn, NY

	Long Island University, Long Island, NY Momentum Institute of Design, Chicago, IL Woodstock Artists Association, NY
1960	YMHA New York, NY Woodstock Artists Association, NY Pratt Institute, Brooklyn, NY
1961	Woodstock Artists Association, NY
1962	Pratt Institute Faculty Shows Brooklyn, NY
1963	Woodstock Artists Association, NY
1964	Pratt Institute Faculty Show, Brooklyn, NY
1965	Chelsea Art Association, NY
1966	Pratt Institute, Brooklyn, NY
1967	Princeton Gallery, NJ
1968-71	Pratt Institute, Brooklyn, NY
1969	Woodstock Artists Association, NY
1971	Suffolk Museum, Stony Brook, NY
1972	Lerner - Miraschi Gallery, NY
1973	Princeton Gallery of Fine Art, NJ
1974	Cornucopia Gallery, Empire State Plaza, Albany, NY Grace Gallery, Brooklyn, NY
1977	Nassau County Community College, Long Island, NY Mickelson Gallery, Washington, DC
1978	*"Work Behind the Work"*, Ulster County Community College, Stone Ridge, NY Princeton Gallery of Fine Art, NJ *29th New England Exhibition of Painting and Sculpture*, Silvermine Gallery, New Canaan, CT
1979	Brooklyn Museum, Brooklyn, NY
1978-80	Center Square Gallery, Albany, NY Sunne Savage Gallery, Boston, MA
1981	Somerhill Gallery, Durham, NC
1982-83	Woodstock School of Art, Woodstock, NY
1983	Ulster County Art Association, Kingston, NY Novo Arts, New York, NY

1986-88	Princeton Gallery of Fine Art, NJ
1988-89	Thompson Gallery, New York, NY
1988	*"Former Faculty Centennial Exhibition"*, Pratt Manhattan Center, Puck Building, Soho, NY
1989	*"Man and His Space"*, The Society of Landscape and Figurative Artists, Lever House, New York, NY Strauss Gallery, New York, NY Bell Gallery, Woodstock, NY
1990	Z Gallery, Soho, NY Schafler Gallery, Pratt Institute, Brooklyn, NY
1991	*"Five Artists"*, Pratt Manhattan Center, Puck Building, Soho, NY Woodstock Artists Association, NY
1992	Park West Gallery, Kingston, NY
1993	Marguerite Oestreicher Fine Art, New Orleans, LA *"Five Artists"*, Haenah Kent, Soho, NY Walter Wickiser Gallery, Inc., Soho, NY
1994	Park West, Kingston, NY Haenah Kent, Seoul, Korea
1995	Woodstock Artists Association
1997	Tallahassee Museum of Natural History, Tallahassee, FL Fernbank Museum of Natural History, Atlanta, GA
1998	Woodstock Guild, Woodstock, NY
1999	Gross McCleaf Gallery, Philadelphia, PA The Cahoon Museum of American Art, Cotuit, MA *"Abstract Expressionism, Expanding the Canon"*, Gary Snyder Fine Art, Chelsea, NY
2005	Art Chicago, Chicago, IL Art Toronto, Toronto, Canada
2010	(REAL)ists, Selby Gallery, Ringling College of Art and Design, Sarasota, FL Art Chicago, Chicago, IL Art Toronto, Toronto, Canada Art Miami, Miami Florida
2011	Art Chicago, Chicago, IL Art Toronto, Toronto, Canada
2012	Art Palm Beach, Palm Beach, Florida ArtHamptons, Bridgehampton, NY

SELECTED PUBLIC COLLECTIONS

Bulbrite Inc., NJ
Currier Gallery, Manchester, NH
Continental Trust Bank, Fort Worth, TX
Eastern Illinois University, Charleston, IL
High Museum, Atlanta, GA
Louisiana State University, Baton Rouge, LA
Lehigh University, Bethlehem, PA
Louisiana Art Commission, Baton Rouge, LA
Mint Museum, Charlotte, NC
New Orleans Museum of Art, New Orleans, LA
Pratt Institute, Brooklyn, NY
United Cerebral Palsy Association of Westchester County, Inc
Woodstock Historical Society, Woodstock, NY

SELECTED PRIVATE COLLECTIONS

Mr. Don Ahn, NY
Mr. Richard Allen, NY
Mr. Robert Allen, NY
Ms. Stephanie Arata, NY
Mr. Sei Arimori, Japan
Ms. Martha Armstrong, MA
Mr. William Breger, NY
Mrs. Kiyoko Ohata Brown, NY
Mr. Song Jun Chon, Korea
Mr. David Cleveland, NY
Mr. Morris Cook, NY
Mr. Nemeir Cortas, London
Mrs. Layla Fanucci, CA
Mr. Robert Feur, Woodside, NY
Mr. & Mrs. Elliot Gruenberg, NY
Mr. Rollins S. Guild, NY
Dr. Lloyd Harris, NY
Mr. Henry Heald, NY
Mr. Fergus Hoke, London
Mrs. Duoling Huang, NY
Mr. Tchah Sup Kim, NY
Mr. & Mrs. Alan Kleiman, NY
Mr. & Mrs. Steven G. Lampe, NY
Ms. Kang Ja Lee, Seoul, Korea
Mr. Daniel E. Muallem, CA
Mr. Vincent Naddeo, NY
Mr. Hiro Nozuka, NY
Mrs. Marguerite Oestricher, LA
Mr. & Mrs. Pearlman, NY
Ms. Ann Rand, NY
Ms. Lina Shamma, London
Mr. & Mrs. Marc Savitt, NY
Mr. & Mrs. Robert Schwagerl, NY
Mr. & Mrs. Jim Stynes, NY
Mr. Peter Ted Surace, NY
Mrs. Kathy Surace-Smith, WA
Mr. Michael Sut, NY
Ms. Bronwin White, LA
Mr. and Mrs. David Worth, NC
Mr. George Zhaozhi Xiong, NY
Ms. Zhang Zhang, Shanghai

AWARDS AND HONORS

1934,39	Louis Comfort Tiffany Fellowship, Oyster Bay, Long Island, NY
1946,48	Louisiana State Research Council Grant, Baton Rouge, LA
1952	Fund for the Advancement of Education Grant
1956	Honorary PhD, Eastern Illinois University, Charleston, IL
1964	Distinguished Alumni Award, Eastern Illinois University, Charleston, IL
1971-75	Harriman College, Member of the Board of Trustees, Harriman, NY
1975	Men of Achievement Award, Melrose Press, Cambridge, UK
1975	Professor Emeritus, Pratt Institute, Brooklyn, NY

COMMISSIONS

1947	Standard Oil of New Jersey, *The American Highway*, Ten colored lithographs reproduced in *The Lamp*, 29, 3, June 1947
1948,49	Ford Company, *Ford Times*, Watercolor Series

TEACHING EXPERIENCE

1941-56	Chairman, Art Department, Louisiana State University, Baton Rouge, LA
1956-59	Director, Division of Art Education, State University, New Paltz, NY
1959-62	Chairman, Art Education Department, Pratt Institute, Brooklyn, NY
1962-75	Director, Division of Graduate Programs in Art and Design, Pratt Institute, Brooklyn, NY
1972	Acting Dean, School of Art and Design, Pratt Institute, Brooklyn, NY
1975-78	Visiting Professor Emeritus of Graduate Art, Pratt Institute, Brooklyn, NY

EDUCATION

1928-31	Art Institute of Chicago
1931-34	BA, Eastern Illinois College
1934-35	MA, Vanderbilt and Peabody
1935-38	PhD, Peabody

Index

CREDITS

Art work photography: John Kleinhans, Woodstock, NY

pages 75, 76, 77, 80, 95, 101, 107, 109, 111

Art work photography: Becket Logan, New York, NY

pages 31, 37, 38, 39, 41, 43, 47, 61, 63, 67, 73, 81,

84, 85, 87, 89, 91, 93, 97, 103, 105, 111, 113, 116, 117

Portrait photography: Patti Ouderkirk, New York, NY

page 23 (Wickiser with Mr. and Mrs. Pace)

Portrait photography: Al Wooley, Baton Rouge, LA

pages 14 (Wickiser printing lithographs), 16